for Lent 2019

SACRED SPACE

from the website www.sacredspace.ie

Prayer from the Irish Jesuits

LOYOLA PRESS.
A JESUIT MINISTRY
Chicago

LOYOLA PRESS.
A JESUIT MINISTRY

3441 N. Ashland Avenue
Chicago, Illinois 60657
(800) 621-1008
www.loyolapress.com

Scripture quotations are from the *New Revised Standard Version Bible: Catholic Edition*, copyright © 1989, 1993 National Council of the Churches of Christ in the United States of America. Used by permission. All rights reserved.

Cover art credit: Charles Harker/Moment/Getty Images.

ISBN: 978-0-8294-4704-0

Printed in the United States of America.
18 19 20 21 22 23 Versa 10 9 8 7 6 5 4 3 2 1

Contents

The Presence of God

Bless all who worship you, almighty God,
from the rising of the sun to its setting:
from your goodness enrich us,
by your love inspire us,
by your Spirit guide us,
by your power protect us,
in your mercy receive us,
now and always.

How to Use This Booklet

During each week of Lent, begin by reading the "Something to think and pray about each day this week." Then proceed through "The Presence of God," "Freedom," and "Consciousness" steps to prepare yourself to hear the Word of God in your heart. In the next step, "The Word," turn to the Scripture reading for each day of the week. Inspiration points are provided if you need them. Then return to the "Conversation" and "Conclusion" steps. Follow this process every day of Lent.

March 6—March 9

Something to think and pray about each day this week:

Every Christian can become a witness to the risen Jesus. And his or her witness is all the more credible, the more it shines through a life lived by the Gospel, a joyful, courageous, gentle, peaceful, merciful life. Instead, if a Christian gives in to ease, vanity, and selfishness, if he or she becomes deaf and blind to the question of "resurrection" of many brothers and sisters, how can [that person] communicate the living Jesus? How can the Christian communicate the freeing power of the living Jesus and his infinite tenderness?

Listen to Jesus. He is the Savior: follow him. To listen to Christ, in fact, entails *taking up the logic of his Pascal Mystery*, setting out on the journey with him to make of oneself a gift of love to others, in docile obedience to the will of God, with an attitude of interior freedom and of detachment from worldly things. One must, in other words, be willing to lose one's very life (cf. Mark 8:35), by giving it up so that all men might be saved; thus, we will meet in eternal happiness. The path to Jesus always leads us to happiness—don't forget it! Jesus' way always leads us to happiness. There will always be a cross, trials in the middle, but at the end we are always led to happiness. Jesus does not deceive us; he promised us happiness and will give it to us if we follow his ways.

—Pope Francis, *Embracing the Way of Jesus*

The Presence of God

"Be still and know that I am God!" Lord, your words lead us to the calmness and greatness of your presence.

Freedom

"In these days, God taught me as a schoolteacher teaches a pupil" (Saint Ignatius). I remind myself that there are things God has to teach me yet, and I ask for the grace to hear them and let them change me.

Consciousness

How am I really feeling? Lighthearted? Heavyhearted? I may be very much at peace, happy to be here. Equally, I may be frustrated, worried, or angry. I acknowledge how I really am. It is the real me whom the Lord loves.

The Word

God speaks to each of us individually. I listen attentively to hear what he is saying to me. Read the text a few times; then listen. (Please turn to the Scripture on the following pages. Inspiration points are there, should you need them. When you are ready, return here to continue.)

Conversation

Do I notice myself reacting as I pray with the word of God? Do I feel challenged, comforted, angry? Imagining Jesus sitting or standing by me, I speak out my feelings, as one trusted friend to another.

Conclusion

I thank God for these moments we have spent together and for any insights I have been given concerning the text.

Wednesday 6th March
Ash Wednesday
Matthew 6:1–6, 16–18

[Jesus said,] "Beware of practicing your piety before others in order to be seen by them; for then you have no reward from your Father in heaven. So whenever you give alms, do not sound a trumpet before you, as the hypocrites do in the synagogues and in the streets, so that they may be praised by others. Truly I tell you, they have received their reward. But when you give alms, do not let your left hand know what your right hand is doing, so that your alms may be done in secret; and your Father who sees in secret will reward you. And whenever you pray, do not be like the hypocrites; for they love to stand and pray in the synagogues and at the street corners, so that they may be seen by others. Truly I tell you, they have received their reward. But whenever you pray, go into your room and shut the door and pray to your Father who is in secret; and your Father who sees in secret will reward you. And whenever you fast, do not look dismal, like the hypocrites, for they disfigure their faces so as to show others that they are fasting. Truly I tell you, they have received their reward. But when you fast, put oil on your head and wash your face, so that your fasting may be seen not by others but by your Father who is in secret; and your Father who sees in secret will reward you."

- What motivates me, deepest down? Do I act solely to please God? Jesus gives hypocrites a hard time. They pretend to be what they are not; they are actors, performing behind their masks. When am I most likely to put up a pretense? Do I ever catch myself telling small lies to give others a better impression of myself?

- I must be content to be who I am. My deepest identity is not the one I create for myself but the identity given me by God. I am the beloved of God, and always will be. That is enough. The important person in my life must be not myself, nor others, but only God who sees in secret. God also knows my secret: when everything is said and done, I am infinitely loved!

Thursday 7th March
Luke 9:22–25

[Jesus said to his disciples:] "The Son of Man must undergo great suffering, and be rejected by the elders, chief priests, and scribes, and be killed, and on the third day be raised." Then he said to them all, "If any want to become my followers, let them deny themselves and take up their cross daily and follow me. For those who want to save their life will lose it, and those who lose their life for my sake will save it. What does it profit them if they gain the whole world, but lose or forfeit themselves?"

- At the start of Lent, Jesus puts before us the central events of his Passion, Death, and Resurrection. Jesus states clearly that his project to save the world will end in disaster for himself. I sit with him in silence and with gratitude that he does not simply give up and abandon humankind to its malice.

- Let me also chat with him about the things I endure. He is not saying that suffering is good, but that I can either accept it patiently or try to reject it. He looks hard at me and says, "You could spend your life just looking after yourself and trying to avoid pain and hurt. Or you can embrace the world with love and risk failure, betrayal, disappointment from those you try to serve. Of course you will get hurt, but an eternal blessing will be yours at the end." I respond: "Lord, let me live my life as you lived yours." He thanks me.

Friday 8th March
Matthew 9:14–15

Then the disciples of John came to Jesus, saying, "Why do we and the Pharisees fast often, but your disciples do not fast?" And Jesus said to them, "The wedding guests cannot mourn as long as the bridegroom is with them, can they? The days will come when the bridegroom is taken away from them, and then they will fast."

- John the Baptist and his disciples have their doubts about Jesus. Devout Jews observed regular obligatory fasts and would also undertake private fasting, by way of praying for God's salvation and hastening the coming of the kingdom. We can often feel like John's disciples, confused and unsure about what to do. The divisions in the Church upset us. But Jesus is saying: "With my coming, a wedding has started; a new creation is under way; be joyful!"

- Jesus wanted to celebrate and socialize with everybody, especially the outcasts, the prodigals, the sinners, to let them know that in him the joyful time of salvation had indeed come. I must stop living in no-man's-land. I must wake up—the Savior of the world has come, and I must join him.

Saturday 9th March
Luke 5:27–32

After this he went out and saw a tax collector named Levi, sitting at the tax booth; and he said to him, "Follow me." And he got up, left everything, and followed him. Then Levi gave a great banquet for him in his house; and there was a large crowd of tax collectors and others sitting at the table with them. The

Pharisees and their scribes were complaining to his disciples, saying, "Why do you eat and drink with tax collectors and sinners?" Jesus answered, "Those who are well have no need of a physician, but those who are sick; I have come to call not the righteous but sinners to repentance."

- Tax collectors were despised: they were social and religious outcasts. Why then does Jesus choose Levi out of all possible candidates? Because he is determined to break down dramatically the barriers that fragment human community. Who are the tax collectors in my world?

- The banquet indicates table fellowship; eating and drinking together shows that the guests accept one another. Since Jesus is the main guest, we are shown that if we want to be with him at the table, we must accept the companionship of people we have despised. At the Eucharist, Jesus invites everyone to participate, not simply as individuals but as fellow disciples who are both sinners and forgiven. Do I complain about this, in words, or silently in my heart?

First Week of Lent
March 10—March 16

Something to think and pray about each day this week:

God's world is a world in which everyone feels responsible for the other, for the good of the other. . . . [I]n reflection, fasting, and prayer, each of us deep down should ask ourselves, Is this really the world I desire? Is this really the world we all carry in our hearts? Is the world that we want really a world of harmony and peace, in ourselves, in our relations with others, in families, in cities, *in* and *between* nations? And does not true freedom mean choosing ways in this world that lead to the good of all and are guided by love? But then we wonder, Is this the world in which we are living? Creation retains its beauty, which fills us with awe, and it remains a good work. But there are also "violence, division, disagreement, war." These occur when man, the summit of creation, stops contemplating beauty and goodness, and withdraws into his own selfishness.

—Pope Francis, *Embracing the Way of Jesus*

The Presence of God
I remind myself that, as I sit here now,
God is gazing on me with love and holding me in being.
I pause for a moment and think of this.

Freedom
"There are very few people who realize what God would make of them if they abandoned themselves into his hands, and let themselves be formed by his grace" (Saint Ignatius). I ask for the grace to trust myself totally to God's love.

Consciousness
Where do I sense hope, encouragement, and growth in my life? By looking back over the past few months, I may be able to see which activities and occasions have produced rich fruit. If I do notice such areas, I will determine to give those areas both time and space in the future.

The Word
Lord Jesus, you became human to communicate with me.
You walked and worked on this earth.
You endured the heat and struggled with the cold.
All your time on this earth was spent in caring for humanity.

You healed the sick, you raised the dead.
Most important of all, you saved me from death.
(Please turn to the Scripture on the following pages.
Inspiration points are there, should you need them.
When you are ready, return here to continue.)

Conversation
What is stirring in me as I pray? Am I consoled, troubled, left cold? I imagine Jesus standing or sitting at my side, and I share my feelings with him.

Conclusion
Glory be to the Father, and to the Son, and to the Holy Spirit,
As it was in the beginning, is now and ever shall be,
World without end. Amen.

Sunday 10th March

Luke 4:1–13

Jesus, full of the Holy Spirit, returned from the Jordan and was led by the Spirit in the wilderness, where for forty days he was tempted by the devil. He ate nothing at all during those days, and when they were over, he was famished. The devil said to him, "If you are the Son of God, command this stone to become a loaf of bread." Jesus answered him, "It is written, 'One does not live by bread alone.'" Then the devil led him up and showed him in an instant all the kingdoms of the world. And the devil said to him, "To you I will give their glory and all this authority; for it has been given over to me, and I give it to anyone I please. If you, then, will worship me, it will all be yours." Jesus answered him, "It is written, 'Worship the Lord your God, and serve only him.'" Then the devil took him to Jerusalem, and placed him on the pinnacle of the temple, saying to him, "If you are the Son of God, throw yourself down from here, for it is written, 'He will command his angels concerning you, to protect you,' and 'On their hands they will bear you up, so that you will not dash your foot against a stone.'" Jesus answered him, "It is said, 'Do not put the Lord your God to the test.'" When the devil had finished every test, he departed from him until an opportune time.

- Lord, you told of these temptations to your disciples—how else would they have known? Can I put words on my own temptations, the particular weaknesses or wickedness that draw me in? Can I see my temptations as you did, against the backdrop of the vocation to which you call me?

- Jesus, like Moses before him, retreats into the wilderness where he fasts for forty days. Each temptation involves a seizure of power: power over the elements of creation by turning stones into bread; political and military power by gaining power over the kingdoms of the world; and the power to force God's protection in an inappropriate manner. That Jesus was tested throughout his ministry was widely held in early Christianity. The letter to the Hebrews tells us, "For do we not have a high priest [Jesus] who is unable to sympathize with our weaknesses, but we have one who in every respect has been tested as we are, yet without sin."

Monday 11th March
Matthew 25:31–46

[Jesus said,] "When the Son of Man comes in his glory, and all the angels with him, then he will sit on the throne of his glory. All the nations will be gathered before him, and he will separate people one from another as a shepherd separates the sheep from the goats, and he will put the sheep at his right hand and the goats at the left. Then the king will say to those at his right hand, 'Come, you that are blessed by my Father, inherit the kingdom prepared for you from the foundation of the world; for I was hungry and you gave me food, I was thirsty and you gave me something to drink, I was a stranger and you welcomed me, I was naked and you gave me clothing, I was sick and you took care of me, I was in prison and you visited me.' Then the righteous will answer him, 'Lord, when was it that we saw you hungry and gave you food, or thirsty and gave you something to drink? And when was it that we saw you a stranger and welcomed you, or naked and gave you clothing? And when was it that we saw you sick or in prison and visited you?' And the king will answer them, 'Truly I tell you, just as you did it to one of the least of these who are members of my family, you did it to me.' Then he will say to those at his left hand, 'You that are accursed, depart from me into the eternal fire prepared for the devil and his angels; for I was hungry and you gave me no food, I was thirsty and you gave me nothing to drink, I was a stranger and you did not welcome me, naked and you did not give me clothing, sick and in prison and you did not visit me.' Then they also will answer, 'Lord, when was it that we saw you hungry or thirsty or a stranger or naked or sick or in prison, and did not take care of you?'

Then he will answer them, 'Truly I tell you, just as you did not do it to one of the least of these, you did not do it to me.' And these will go away into eternal punishment, but the righteous into eternal life."

- Each group goes to the place it has chosen. Those whose lives were oriented to love and mercy come to the love and mercy of God. Those who excluded people in need from their lives have excluded themselves from God's kingdom, where there is only acceptance and love. What place do I choose through my priorities and actions this day?

- This parable of the sheep and the goats is not about the future, but about opening my eyes here and now to the needs of my neighbor: the hungry, the homeless, the refugee, the isolated lonely ones. Jesus identifies with each one. If I turn away from my brothers and sisters in need, I am turning away from my brother Jesus.

Tuesday 12th March
Matthew 6:7–15

[Jesus said to his disciples,] "When you are praying, do not heap up empty phrases as the Gentiles do; for they think that they will be heard because of their many words. Do not be like them, for your Father knows what you need before you ask him. Pray then in this way:

"Our Father in heaven,
hallowed be your name.
Your kingdom come.
Your will be done,
on earth as it is in heaven.
Give us this day our daily bread.
And forgive us our debts,
as we also have forgiven our debtors.
And do not bring us to the time of trial,
but rescue us from the evil one."

- God knows what I need before I ask. When, then, should I ask? Do you want me to hear for myself what I need, Lord? Do you long for conversation with me? Do you wait for me to rely on you and turn to you for what I need?

- When are my words "empty phrases"? How do I know when my prayer does not have meaningful content? How do I feel when prayer has become empty? I spend time recalling how I have experienced prayer at different times. Holy Spirit, show me what I need to see.

Wednesday 13th March
Luke 11:29–32

When the crowds were increasing, he began to say, "This generation is an evil generation; it asks for a sign, but no sign will be given to it except the sign of Jonah. For just as Jonah became a sign to the people of Nineveh, so the Son of Man will be to this generation. The queen of the South will rise at the judgment with the people of this generation and condemn them, because she came from the ends of the earth to listen to the wisdom of Solomon, and see, something greater than Solomon is here! The people of Nineveh will rise up at the judgment with this generation and condemn it, because they repented at the proclamation of Jonah, and see, something greater than Jonah is here!"

- The Ninevites were moved to repentance by the prophetic sign of Jonah, which they recognized as the authentic word of God. Later, God sends his Son into our world as the ultimate sign of his love for us. You, Lord Jesus, are the sign of signs. Those who go seeking further wonders have not truly seen you. In you I find all that I need to be fully human and to find my destiny with God.

- Jesus uses imagination, trying to help his audience catch on to the mystery of who he is. So, he reminds them of famous characters in stories they already know well. He then tries to open their minds further by saying twice that "something greater" is here in his person. Do I cultivate my capacity for mystery, or do I live on the surface of life? Do I reduce the wonders of nature and of the cosmos to mere facts, or do I let myself be drawn to wonder what their author must be like? Everything is a divine mystery because all comes from God. Let me sit with Jesus and ask him to enliven the mystical dimension that may be dormant in me.

Thursday 14th March
Matthew 7:7–12

[Jesus said to his disciples,] "Ask, and it will be given to you; search, and you will find; knock, and the door will be opened for you. For everyone who asks receives, and everyone who searches finds, and for everyone who knocks, the door will be opened. Is there anyone among you who, if your child asks for bread, will give a stone? Or if the child asks for a fish, will give a snake? If you then, who are evil, know how to give good gifts to your children, how much more will your Father in heaven give good things to those who ask him!"

- In the very act of praying we receive something from God. As we open our hearts to God in prayer, God's hands are open to give us good gifts. We leave a time of prayer with an increase of faith, hope, and love, which is the consolation of God. No time of prayer is wasted; all prayer is in the service of love, and prayer increases within us our capacity to love.

- God welcomes me with a loving embrace, and desires to give me "good things" when I ask him with a sincere and open heart. Am I truly open with God in my prayer? Do I share with him all that I am living, my struggles and my joys, and the concrete situations for which I need his help?

Friday 15th March
Matthew 5:20–26

For I tell you, unless your righteousness exceeds that of the scribes and Pharisees, you will never enter the kingdom of heaven. You have heard that it was said to those of ancient times, "You shall not murder"; and "whoever murders shall be liable to judgment." But I say to you that if you are angry with a brother or sister, you will be liable to judgment; and if you insult a brother or sister, you will be liable to the council; and if you say, "You fool," you will be liable to the hell of fire. So when you are offering your gift at the altar, if you remember that your brother or sister has something against you, leave your gift there before the altar and go; first be reconciled to your brother or sister, and then come and offer your gift. Come to terms quickly with your accuser while you are on the way to court with him, or your accuser may hand you over to the judge, and the judge to the guard, and you will be thrown into prison. Truly I tell you, you will never get out until you have paid the last penny.

- The standards operating in the kingdom of heaven are high! Jesus does not dismiss Old Testament teaching but goes to the root of things. We can be smug and content with our conventional good behavior. However, Jesus says to us, "But what about your anger? What about insulting someone? Do you despise anyone, ever? Such behavior won't do anymore."

- Is there anybody I need to forgive? I pray for the grace to forgive that person in my heart and fully let go of any feelings of anger or resentment I may have toward him or her. I ask the Lord for the grace to go to that person and be reconciled with him or her and, if possible, restore the relationship to one of friendship and love.

Saturday 16th March
Matthew 5:43–48

[Jesus said,] "You have heard that it was said, 'You shall love your neighbor and hate your enemy.' But I say to you, Love your enemies and pray for those who persecute you, so that you may be children of your Father in heaven; for he makes his sun rise on the evil and on the good, and sends rain on the righteous and on the unrighteous. For if you love those who love you, what reward do you have? Do not even the tax collectors do the same? And if you greet only your brothers and sisters, what more are you doing than others? Do not even the Gentiles do the same? Be perfect, therefore, as your heavenly Father is perfect."

- Loving our enemies is among the most challenging precepts taught by Jesus. Notice how he finds motivation and a standard in the love shown by our Father in heaven: a love that is all-embracing, indiscriminate, inclusive. Modeling our love on that of the Father is the way to be perfect.

- Contemplate the wonder of God's unconditional love for you and ask for the grace to radiate that love in the different situations and activities of your day.

March 17—March 23

Something to think and pray about each day this week:

Something stirred from deep within. I felt it knocking, begging to be acknowledged and released. I could not put a name to it, but something felt awakened after a long period of dormancy. In truth, this gnawing sensation had been building for more than a year, but on the levee that day, I grappled with this powerful presence at work in me. I had no words for the hunger that was asking me for more. All I could do was attempt to be still and acknowledge its existence. I took a deep breath and looked to God above, begging for help with what felt like an insurmountable task: sitting still and being quiet. Slowly, as the deep breaths continued, inner stillness came. I began to notice my surroundings. In that moment, I saw everything as it was—beautiful, holy, God's gift. My heart welled to the point that I thought it would leap out of my chest. I realized that the hunger I felt was my desire for God. For one solid hour, I breathed deeply in the silence and in being with God. On that day, I touched something powerful: God within me, residing in the inner space that only God and I can access. I understood that holiness lived within me as much as it lived outside me in the beautiful surroundings of the retreat grounds.

—Becky Eldredge, *Busy Lives & Restless Souls*

The Presence of God
I pause for a moment
and reflect on God's life-giving presence
in every part of my body,
in everything around me,
in the whole of my life.

Freedom
Many countries are at this moment suffering the agonies of war. I bow my head in thanksgiving for my freedom. I pray for all prisoners and captives.

Consciousness
Knowing that God loves me unconditionally, I look honestly over the past day, its events, and my feelings. Do I have something to be grateful for? Then I give thanks. Is there something I am sorry for? Then I ask forgiveness.

The Word
Now I turn to the Scripture set out for me this day. I read slowly over the words and see if any sentence or sentiment appeals to me. (Please turn to the Scripture on the following pages. Inspiration points are there, should you need them. When you are ready, return here to continue.)

Conversation

I know with certainty that there were times when you carried me, Lord. There were times when it was through your strength that I got through the dark times in my life.

Conclusion

Glory be to the Father, and to the Son, and to the Holy Spirit,
As it was in the beginning, is now and ever shall be,
World without end. Amen.

Sunday 17th March

Luke 9:28b–36

Now about eight days after these sayings Jesus took with him Peter and John and James, and went up on the mountain to pray. And while he was praying, the appearance of his face changed, and his clothes became dazzling white. Suddenly they saw two men, Moses and Elijah, talking to him. They appeared in glory and were speaking of his departure, which he was about to accomplish at Jerusalem. Now Peter and his companions were weighed down with sleep; but since they had stayed awake, they saw his glory and the two men who stood with him. Just as they were leaving him, Peter said to Jesus, "Master, it is good for us to be here; let us make three dwellings, one for you, one for Moses, and one for Elijah"—not knowing what he said. While he was saying this, a cloud came and overshadowed them; and they were terrified as they entered the cloud. Then from the cloud came a voice that said, "This is my Son, my Chosen; listen to him!" When the voice had spoken, Jesus was found alone. And they kept silent and in those days told no one any of the things they had seen.

- Peter and John and James were privileged to see Jesus in his full dignity. We can see one another in the same way, with the enlightenment of the Holy Spirit. At all sacramental moments, we see those we love in their true dignity as human beings beloved of God. The dreams for this perfect infant at baptism, the blessing with gifts at confirmation, the beauty of forgiveness at reconciliation, the warmth of communion, the hope for healing at the sacrament of the anointing of the sick, the dignity of covenant love at matrimony, the beauty of service at ordination. Fine clothing sometimes makes us even gasp with admiration.

- When have your eyes been opened to the full dignity of another person? Recall that moment and savor it, thanking God for the gift of his vision.

Monday 18th March
Luke 6:36–38

[Jesus said to the disciples,] "Be merciful, just as your Father is merciful. Do not judge, and you will not be judged; do not condemn, and you will not be condemned. Forgive, and you will be forgiven; give, and it will be given to you. A good measure, pressed down, shaken together, running over, will be put into your lap; for the measure you give will be the measure you get back."

- Jesus invites us to be as God is—nothing less! He does not intend to overwhelm us or cause us to feel frustrated by such an enormous invitation; he wants us to wonder at the immensity of God's capacity to love. In our humanity, we are not infinite, but we are called to great love and hope. The invitation reaches to us *as we are*, calling us into the life of God.

- Judgment, condemnation, and lack of forgiveness inhibit good and bind up the spirit. Lord, help me to be generous, not by forcing anything from myself but by sharing fully what you give to me.

Tuesday 19th March
Saint Joseph, Spouse of the Blessed Virgin Mary
Matthew 1:16, 18–21, 24

Jacob was the father of Joseph the husband of Mary, of whom Jesus was born, who is called the Messiah. Now the birth of Jesus the Messiah took place in this way. When his mother Mary had been engaged to Joseph, but before they lived together, she was found to be with child from the Holy Spirit. Her husband Joseph, being a righteous man and unwilling to expose her to public disgrace, planned to dismiss her quietly. But just when he had resolved to do this, an angel of the Lord appeared to him in a dream and said, "Joseph, son of David, do not be afraid to take Mary as your wife, for the child conceived in her is from the Holy Spirit. She will bear a son, and you are to name him Jesus, for he will save his people from their sins." When Joseph awoke from sleep, he did as the angel of the Lord commanded him; he took her as his wife.

- What do we know about St. Joseph? That he loved Mary so much that he suppressed his doubts about her chastity and allowed himself to be regarded as the father of her child, knowing that he wasn't (when Jesus took the floor in the Nazareth synagogue, the begrudgers remarked: "Is not this the son of Joseph?"); that he brought up that child as his own, despite great difficulties and dangers, particularly at the start; that he taught him his trade; that he loved him; and that Jesus' robust health as an adult (physical stamina, courage, strength of purpose, and attractiveness to women, men, and children) is proof of good parenting by his foster father. Joseph is the obvious patron of adoptive fathers.

- I pray for all the men I know who are foster fathers, stepfathers, adoptive fathers, single fathers, and father figures to others.

Wednesday 20th March
Matthew 20:17–28

While Jesus was going up to Jerusalem, he took the twelve disciples aside by themselves, and said to them on the way, "See, we are going up to Jerusalem, and the Son of Man will be handed over to the chief priests and scribes, and they will condemn him to death; then they will hand him over to the Gentiles to be mocked and flogged and crucified; and on the third day he will be raised." Then the mother of the sons of Zebedee came to him with her sons, and kneeling before him, she asked a favor of him. And he said to her, "What do you want?" She said to him, "Declare that these two sons of mine will sit, one at your right hand and one at your left, in your kingdom." But Jesus answered, "You do not know what you are asking. Are you able to drink the cup that I am about to drink?" They said to him, "We are able." He said to them, "You will indeed drink my cup, but to sit at my right hand and at my left, this is not mine to grant, but it is for those for whom it has been prepared by my Father." When the ten heard it, they were angry with the two brothers. But Jesus called them to him and said, "You know that the rulers of the Gentiles lord it over them, and their great ones are tyrants over them. It will not be so among you; but whoever wishes to be great among you must be your servant, and whoever wishes to be first among you must be your slave; just as the Son of Man came not to be served but to serve, and to give his life a ransom for many."

- Our prayer often finds us asking for what we want. As we grow in awareness of the presence of God, we realize how God wants for us something greater. It may appear that we are asked to let go of our requests, but we soon realize that nothing we really want is lost in God.

- Jesus was clear about his relationship with God; he knew who he was and what was his to give. Lord, help me know more clearly what is mine to do and what I might best leave to you.

Thursday 21st March
Luke 16:19–31

[Jesus said to the Pharisees,] "There was a rich man who was dressed in purple and fine linen and who feasted sumptuously every day. And at his gate lay a poor man named Lazarus, covered with sores, who longed to satisfy his hunger with what fell from the rich man's table; even the dogs would come and lick his sores. The poor man died and was carried away by the angels to be with Abraham. The rich man also died and was buried. In Hades, where he was being tormented, he looked up and saw Abraham far away with Lazarus by his side. He called out, 'Father Abraham, have mercy on me, and send Lazarus to dip the tip of his finger in water and cool my tongue; for I am in agony in these flames.' But Abraham said,

'Child, remember that during your lifetime you received your good things, and Lazarus in like manner evil things; but now he is comforted here, and you are in agony. Besides all this, between you and us a great chasm has been fixed, so that those who might want to pass from here to you cannot do so, and no one can cross from there to us.' He said, 'Then, father, I beg you to send him to my father's house—for I have five brothers—that he may warn them, so that they will not also come into this place of torment.' Abraham replied, 'They have Moses and the prophets; they should listen to them.' He said, 'No, father Abraham; but if someone goes to them from the dead, they will repent.' He said to him, 'If they do not listen to Moses and the prophets, neither will they be convinced even if someone rises from the dead.'"

- Take some time to speak to Jesus about this story; consider the situation that was in his mind and recognize how his heart was moved. Look, with Jesus, at your situation, at your world: Who are the self-satisfied rich, who are the overlooked poor?

- Jesus describes Lazarus as being forgotten by people, cared for only by dogs. The wealthy in our world often lavish more care on pets than on their brothers and sisters. I ask God to open my heart and to help me look with compassion on the poor so that I become more like Jesus.

Friday 22nd March
Matthew 21:33–43, 45–46

[Jesus said,] "Listen to another parable. There was a landowner who planted a vineyard, put a fence around it, dug a wine press in it, and built a watchtower. Then he leased it to tenants and went to another country. When the harvest time had come, he sent his slaves to the tenants to collect his produce. But the tenants seized his slaves and beat one, killed another, and stoned another. Again he sent other slaves, more than the first; and they treated them in the same way. Finally he sent his son to them, saying, 'They will respect my son.' But when the tenants saw the son, they said to themselves, 'This is the heir; come, let us kill him and get his inheritance.' So they seized him, threw him out of the vineyard, and killed him. Now when the owner of the vineyard comes, what will he do to those tenants?" They said to him, "He will put those wretches to a miserable death, and lease the vineyard to other tenants who will give him the produce at the harvest time." Jesus said to them, "Have you never read in the scriptures: 'The stone that the builders rejected has become the cornerstone; this was the Lord's doing, and it is amazing in our eyes'? Therefore I tell you, the kingdom of God will be taken away from you and given to a people that produces the fruits of the kingdom." . . . When the chief priests and the Pharisees heard his parables, they realized that he was speaking about them. They wanted to arrest him, but they feared the crowds, because they regarded him as a prophet.

- Jesus speaks about the landlord whose absence causes the tenants to forget themselves. I pray for all those who overlook signs of God's care and imagine God's absence; may my prayer for them and my action this day witness to God's presence and love.

- Jesus—the Son—comes to us so that we might receive our inheritance; we do not need to take anything by force but can trust in Jesus' promise, message, and presence.

Saturday 23rd March
Luke 15:1–3, 11–32

Now all the tax collectors and sinners were coming near to listen to him. And the Pharisees and the scribes were grumbling and saying, "This fellow welcomes sinners and eats with them." So he told them this parable: . . . "There was a man who had two sons. The younger of them said to his father, 'Father, give me the share of the property that will belong to me.' So he divided his property between them. A few days later the younger son gathered all he had and traveled to a distant country, and there he squandered his property in dissolute living. When he had spent everything, a severe famine took place throughout that country, and he began to be in need. So he went and hired himself out to one of the citizens of that country, who sent him to his fields to feed the pigs. He would gladly have filled himself with the pods that the pigs were eating; and no one gave him anything. But when he came to himself he said, 'How many of my father's hired hands have bread enough and to spare, but here I am dying of hunger! I will get up and go to my father, and I will say to him, "Father, I have sinned against heaven and before you; I am no longer worthy to be called your son; treat me like one of your hired hands."' So he set off and went to his father. But while he was still far off, his father saw him and was filled with compassion; he ran and put his arms around him and kissed him. Then the son said to him, 'Father, I have sinned against heaven and before you; I am no longer worthy to be called your son.' But the father said to his slaves, 'Quickly, bring out a robe—the best one—and put it on him; put a ring on his finger and sandals on his feet. And get the fatted calf and kill it, and let us eat and celebrate; for this son of mine was dead and is alive again; he was lost and is found!' And they began to celebrate. Now his elder son was in the field; and when he came and approached the house, he heard music and dancing. He called one of the slaves and asked what was going on. He replied, 'Your brother has come, and your father has killed the fatted calf, because he has got him back safe and sound.' Then he became angry and refused to go in. His father came out and began to plead with him. But he answered his father, 'Listen! For all these years I have been working like a slave for you, and I have never disobeyed your command; yet you have never given me even a young goat so that I might celebrate with my friends. But when this son of yours came back, who has devoured your property with prostitutes, you killed the fatted calf for him!' Then the father said to him, 'Son, you are always with me, and all that is mine is yours. But we had to celebrate and rejoice, because this brother of yours was dead and has come to life; he was lost and has been found.'"

- This story is often told to highlight forgiveness or to focus on our need for repentance. It seems that Jesus told it so that we might relish God's abiding mercy. The loving Father desires only to bless and to restore to love and dignity.

- Lord, help me, this Lent, not to focus entirely on my sin but to keep my heart fixed on your love. Don't let me be distracted by any false image of myself, but allow me to hear your invitation to grow in your image, to reflect your love.

March 24—March 30

Something to think and pray about each day this week:

You may ask yourself, *Why don't I have a relationship with God?* or *Am I too late?* You may think to yourself, *I've been away for a long time* or *I want to go deeper.* Wherever you are on your faith journey, fear not. Rest assured of this: God desires a true and intimate relationship with you. Pope Francis implores us to understand that God is waiting for us: "When you have the strength to say, 'I want to come home,' you will find the door open. God will come to meet you because he is always waiting for you—God is always waiting for you. God embraces you, kisses you, and celebrates." I invite you now to reflect on your life. Do you notice a sense of restlessness? Do you feel a hunger for something more? Do you desire a relationship with God but don't know where to start? Do you wonder how God can show up in the everyday details of the normal life you live? God wants to spend time with us, and we can start sharing that time with God today.

—Becky Eldredge, *Busy Lives & Restless Souls*

The Presence of God

I pause for a moment and think of the love and the grace that God showers on me. I am created in the image and likeness of God; I am God's dwelling place.

Freedom

Lord, you granted me the great gift of freedom. In these times, O Lord, grant that I may be free from any form of racism or intolerance. Remind me that we are all equal in your loving eyes.

Consciousness

Knowing that God loves me unconditionally, I can afford to be honest about how I am.

How has the day been, and how do I feel now? I share my feelings openly with the Lord.

The Word

I take my time to read the word of God slowly, a few times, allowing myself to dwell on anything that strikes me. (Please turn to the Scripture on the following pages. Inspiration points are there, should you need them. When you are ready, return here to continue.)

Conversation
Sometimes I wonder what I might say if I were to meet you in person, Lord. I think I might say "Thank you" because you are always there for me.

Conclusion
I thank God for these moments we have spent together and for any insights I have been given concerning the text.

Sunday 24th March

John 4:5–15, 19b–26, 39a, 40–42

So he came to a Samaritan city called Sychar, near the plot of ground that Jacob had given to his son Joseph. Jacob's well was there, and Jesus, tired out by his journey, was sitting by the well. It was about noon. A Samaritan woman came to draw water, and Jesus said to her, "Give me a drink." (His disciples had gone to the city to buy food.) The Samaritan woman said to him, "How is it that you, a Jew, ask a drink of me, a woman of Samaria?" (Jews do not share things in common with Samaritans.) Jesus answered her, "If you knew the gift of God, and who it is that is saying to you, 'Give me a drink,' you would have asked him, and he would have given you living water." The woman said to him, "Sir, you have no bucket, and the well is deep. Where do you get that living water? Are you greater than our ancestor Jacob, who gave us the well, and with his sons and his flocks drank from it?" Jesus said to her, "Everyone who drinks of this water will be thirsty again, but those who drink of the water that I will give them will never be thirsty. The water that I will give will become in them a spring of water gushing up to eternal life." The woman said to him, "Sir, give me this water, so that I may never be thirsty or have to keep coming here to draw water. . . . I see that you are a prophet. Our ancestors worshiped on this mountain, but you say that the place where people must worship is in Jerusalem." Jesus said to her, "Woman, believe me, the hour is coming when you will worship the Father neither on this mountain nor in Jerusalem. You worship what you do not know; we worship what we know, for salvation is from the Jews. But the hour is coming, and is now here, when the true worshipers will worship the Father in spirit and truth, for the Father seeks such as these to worship him. God is spirit, and those who worship him must worship in spirit and truth." The woman said to him, "I know that Messiah is coming" (who is called Christ). "When he comes, he will proclaim all things to us." Jesus said to her, "I am he, the one who is speaking to you." . . . Many Samaritans from that city believed in him because of the woman's testimony. . . . So when the Samaritans came to him, they asked him to stay with them; and he stayed there for two days. And many more believed because of his word. They said to the woman, "It is no longer because of what you said that we believe, for we have heard for ourselves, and we know that this is truly the Savior of the world."

- The thought of Jesus sitting alone by the well is an invitation to be with him. As he looked at the woman, he looks at me: he longs to offer me life; he invites me to see the deeper meaning in what I do; he respects my dignity, asking me to do what I can for him.

- When Jesus says, "If you knew . . . ," he reveals his desire to draw us into knowing God as he does. His open and generous heart is the heart of God, inviting us all to rest where we are known and loved, to find enduring life and lasting refreshment.

Monday 25th March
The Annunciation of the Lord
Luke 1:26–38

In the sixth month the angel Gabriel was sent by God to a town in Galilee called Nazareth, to a virgin engaged to a man whose name was Joseph, of the house of David. The virgin's name was Mary. And he came to her and said, "Greetings, favored one! The Lord is with you." But she was much perplexed by his words and pondered what sort of greeting this might be. The angel said to her, "Do not be afraid, Mary, for you have found favor with God. And now, you will conceive in your womb and bear a son, and you will name him Jesus. He will be great, and will be called the Son of the Most High, and the Lord God will give to him the throne of his ancestor David. He will reign over the house of Jacob for ever, and of his kingdom there will be no end." Mary said to the angel, "How can this be, since I am a virgin?" The angel said to her, "The Holy Spirit will come upon you, and the power of the Most High will overshadow you; therefore the child to be born will be holy; he will be called Son of God. And now, your relative Elizabeth in her old age has also conceived a son; and this is the sixth month for her who was said to be barren. For nothing will be impossible with God." Then Mary said, "Here am I, the servant of the Lord; let it be with me according to your word." Then the angel departed from her.

- As Christians we hope for great things, humanly impossible things, for ourselves individually, for the church and society. As we ask insistently, we remember that "nothing will be impossible with God."

- If things are difficult for me now, I try to say with Mary, "Let it be with me according to your word."

Tuesday 26th March
Matthew 18:21–35

Then Peter came and said to him, "Lord, if another member of the church sins against me, how often should I forgive? As many as seven times?" Jesus said to him, "Not seven times, but, I tell you, seventy-seven times. For this reason the kingdom of heaven may be compared to a king who wished to settle accounts with his slaves. When he began the reckoning, one who owed him ten thousand talents was brought to him; and, as he could not pay, his lord ordered him to be sold, together with his wife and children and all his possessions, and payment to be made. So the slave fell on his knees before him, saying, 'Have patience with me, and I will pay you everything.' And out of pity for him, the lord of that slave released him and forgave him the debt. But that same slave, as he went out, came upon one of his fellow slaves who owed him a hundred denarii; and seizing him by the throat, he said, 'Pay what you owe.' Then his fellow slave fell down and pleaded with him, 'Have patience with me, and I will pay you.' But he refused; then he went and threw him into prison until he would pay the debt. When his fellow slaves saw what had happened, they were greatly distressed, and they went and reported to their lord all that had taken place. Then his lord summoned him and said to him, 'You wicked slave! I forgave you all that debt because you pleaded with me. Should you not have had mercy on your fellow slave, as I had mercy on you?' And in anger his lord handed him over to be tortured until he would pay his entire debt. So my heavenly Father will also do to every one of you, if you do not forgive your brother or sister from your heart."

- Forgiveness can be very hard. C. S. Lewis wrote: "Everyone says forgiveness is a lovely idea, until they have something to forgive." But when I fail to forgive, I am shackled to the evil that has been done to me. I cannot move forward. How free am I this moment? What resentments tie me up?

- If we must be prepared to forgive seventy-seven times, then we must also be ready to ask for forgiveness—and believe we are forgiven—seventy-seven times. When was the last time I asked for forgiveness? I ask the Lord to help me search my heart for any unfinished business.

Wednesday 27th March
Matthew 5:17–19

[Jesus said to the crowds,] "Do not think that I have come to abolish the law or the prophets; I have come not to abolish but to fulfill. For truly I tell you, until heaven and earth pass away, not one letter, not one stroke of a letter, will pass from the law until all is accomplished. Therefore, whoever breaks one of the least of these commandments, and teaches others to do the same, will be called least in the kingdom of heaven; but whoever does them and teaches them will be called great in the kingdom of heaven."

- Lord, you criticized the petty regulations that had been added to the law of God. You summed up the law and the prophets in the love of God and our neighbor. You were not turning your back on the past but deepening our sense of where we stand before God: not as scrupulous rule keepers, but as loving children.

• End your prayer with the writer of the Psalms: "Make me to know your ways, O LORD; teach me your paths. Lead me in your truth, and teach me, for you are the God of my salvation" (Psalm 25:4–5).

Thursday 28th March
Luke 11:14–23

[Jesus] was casting out a demon that was mute; when the demon had gone out, the one who had been mute spoke, and the crowds were amazed. But some of them said, "He casts out demons by Beelzebul, the ruler of the demons." Others, to test him, kept demanding from him a sign from heaven. But he knew what they were thinking and said to them, "Every kingdom divided against itself becomes a desert, and house falls on house. If Satan also is divided against himself, how will his kingdom stand?—for you say that I cast out the demons by Beelzebul. Now if I cast out the demons by Beelzebul, by whom do your exorcists cast them out? Therefore they will be your judges. But if it is by the finger of God that I cast out the demons, then the kingdom of God has come to you. When a strong man, fully armed, guards his castle, his property is safe. But when one stronger than he attacks him and overpowers him, he takes away his armor in which he trusted and divides his plunder. Whoever is not with me is against me, and whoever does not gather with me scatters."

- You know how painful it is if your motives are misunderstood, if a twisted interpretation is put on your good intentions. Such experiences help you identify with Jesus and feel with him. Be there with him; share your experiences with him.

- Some listeners, who have just witnessed Jesus curing a mute man, refuse to think well of him, and invent a slanderous story. It prods me: Do I think ill of others more readily than I credit them with good? Lord, give me the grace to see the best in others, as I'd wish them to see the best in me.

Friday 29th March
Mark 12:28–34

One of the scribes came near and heard them disputing with one another, and seeing that he answered them well, he asked him, "Which commandment is the first of all?" Jesus answered, "The first is, 'Hear, O Israel: the Lord our God, the Lord is one; you shall love the Lord your God with all your heart, and with all your soul, and with all your mind, and with all your strength.' The second is this, 'You shall love your neighbor as yourself.' There is no other commandment greater than these." Then the scribe said to him, "You are right, Teacher; you have truly said that 'he is one, and besides him there is no other'; and 'to love him with all the heart, and with all the understanding, and with all the strength,' and 'to love one's neighbor as oneself,'—this is much more important than all whole burnt offerings and sacrifices." When Jesus saw that he answered wisely, he said to him, "You are not far from the kingdom of God." After that no one dared to ask him any question.

- Why with all our hearts? Because that is the way the Lord loves us. Parents and grandparents have their children constantly on their minds. They are concerned for them even when they are separated geographically. You are ever in God's mind.

- The second commandment, "You shall love your neighbor as yourself," makes your love of God real. "Those who do not love a brother or sister whom they have seen, cannot love God whom they have not seen" (1 John 4:20). Lord Jesus, keep teaching me to love.

Saturday 30th March
Luke 18:9–14

[Jesus] also told this parable to some who trusted in themselves that they were righteous and regarded others with contempt: "Two men went up to the temple to pray, one a Pharisee and the other a tax collector. The Pharisee, standing by himself, was praying thus, 'God, I thank you that I am not like other people: thieves, rogues, adulterers, or even like this tax collector. I fast twice a week; I give a tenth of all my income.' But the tax collector, standing far off, would not even look up to heaven, but was beating his breast and saying, 'God, be merciful to me, a sinner!' I tell you, this man went down to his home justified rather than the other; for all who exalt themselves will be humbled, but all who humble themselves will be exalted."

- Can I ever get rid completely of the Pharisee in me? I find it so easy to feel superior to others in one way or another while being blind to my own shortcomings. Only by making my own the humble prayer of the publican can I be protected from this danger: "God, be merciful to me, a sinner!"

- How does the story hit me? I would hate to be the object of people's contempt. But Lord, if they knew me as you do, they might be right to feel contempt. And I have no right to look down on those whose sins are paraded in the media. Be merciful to me.

Fourth Week of Lent
March 31—April 6

Something to think and pray about each day this week:

We need to know that we can access God at any time and in any place. We carry a chapel within us—a sacred space—and we can call on God at any moment. God is a friend we can talk to throughout the day: as we wake, as we cook, as we eat, as we drive/commute to work, as we play and hang out with our friends. God is available to talk to us as we do laundry, change diapers, run carpool, shuffle kids to activities, oversee homework, and coordinate our families' calendars. *Everything* is holy because our days hold a multitude of ways God can break in and point us back to God as we ponder, pray, and consider.

—Becky Eldredge, *Busy Lives & Restless Souls*

The Presence of God

I pause for a moment and think of the love and the grace that God showers on me. I am created in the image and likeness of God; I am God's dwelling place.

Freedom

Lord, you granted me the great gift of freedom. In these times, O Lord, grant that I may be free from any form of racism or intolerance. Remind me that we are all equal in your loving eyes.

Consciousness

Knowing that God loves me unconditionally, I can afford to be honest about how I am.
How has the day been, and how do I feel now? I share my feelings openly with the Lord.

The Word

I take my time to read the word of God slowly, a few times, allowing myself to dwell on anything that strikes me. (Please turn to the Scripture on the following pages. Inspiration points are there, should you need them. When you are ready, return here to continue.)

Conversation
Sometimes I wonder what I might say if I were to meet you in person, Lord. I think I might say "Thank you" because you are always there for me.

Conclusion
I thank God for these moments we have spent together and for any insights I have been given concerning the text.

Sunday 31st March

John 9:1, 6–9, 13–17, 34–38

As he walked along, he saw a man blind from birth. . . . [Jesus] spat on the ground and made mud with the saliva and spread the mud on the man's eyes, saying to him, "Go, wash in the pool of Siloam" (which means Sent). Then he went and washed and came back able to see. The neighbors and those who had seen him before as a beggar began to ask, "Is this not the man who used to sit and beg?" Some were saying, "It is he." Others were saying, "No, but it is someone like him." He kept saying, "I am the man." . . . They brought to the Pharisees the man who had formerly been blind. Now it was a sabbath day when Jesus made the mud and opened his eyes. Then the Pharisees also began to ask him how he had received his sight. He said to them, "He put mud on my eyes. Then I washed, and now I see." Some of the Pharisees said, "This man is not from God, for he does not observe the sabbath." But others said, "How can a man who is a sinner perform such signs?" And they were divided. So they said again to the blind man, "What do you say about him? It was your eyes he opened." He said, "He is a prophet." . . . They answered him, "You were born entirely in sins, and are you trying to teach us?" And they drove him out. Jesus heard that they had driven him out, and when he found him, he said, "Do you believe in the Son of Man?" He answered, "And who is he, sir? Tell me, so that I may believe in him." Jesus said to him, "You have seen him, and the one speaking with you is he." He said, "Lord, I believe." And he worshiped him.

- The blind man not only receives his sight but the courage to acknowledge what Jesus has done for him: "I am the man." In the full story in John 9:1–38, when the Pharisees argue with him about how Jesus is a sinner breaking the law by healing on the Sabbath, he fearlessly replies, "He is a prophet." Finally, when he is driven out of the temple and Jesus goes looking for him, we hear him say, "Lord, I believe." He now sees with the eyes of faith as well.

- Ask the Lord to give you courage to witness to your faith: sometimes seriously, other times humorously! "Always be ready to make your defense to anyone who demands from you an accounting for the hope that is in you, yet do it with gentleness and reverence" (1 Peter 3:15–16).

Monday 1st April
John 4:43–54

When the two days were over, he went from that place to Galilee (for Jesus himself had testified that a prophet has no honor in the prophet's own country).

When he came to Galilee, the Galileans welcomed him, since they had seen all that he had done in Jerusalem at the festival; for they too had gone to the festival. Then he came again to Cana in Galilee where he had changed the water into wine. Now there was a royal official whose son lay ill in Capernaum. When he heard that Jesus had come from Judea to Galilee, he went and begged him to come down and heal his son, for he was at the point of death. Then Jesus said to him, "Unless you see signs and wonders you will not believe." The official said to him, "Sir, come down before my little boy dies." Jesus said to him, "Go; your son will live." The man believed the word that Jesus spoke to him and started on his way. As he was going down, his slaves met him and told him that his child was alive. So he asked them the hour when he began to recover, and they said to him, "Yesterday at one in the afternoon the fever left him." The father realized that this was the hour when Jesus had said to him, "Your son will live." So he himself believed, along with his whole household. Now this was the second sign that Jesus did after coming from Judea to Galilee.

- Think of the sick people for whom you have prayed. Perhaps your prayer and that of others played its part in their recovery—or had no visible result. Yet no prayer is made in vain. Prayer for another strengthens bonds, softens hearts, and is heard by God.

- For whom do I want to pray now? I trust that the Lord will answer my prayer in the way that is best.

Tuesday 2nd April
John 5:1–16

After this there was a festival of the Jews, and Jesus went up to Jerusalem. Now in Jerusalem by the Sheep Gate there is a pool, called in Hebrew Beth-zatha, which has five porticoes. In these lay many invalids—blind, lame, and paralyzed. One man was there who had been ill for thirty-eight years. When Jesus saw him lying there and knew that he had been there a long time, he said to him, "Do you want to be made well?" The sick man answered him, "Sir, I have no one to put me into the pool when the water is stirred up; and while I am making my way, someone else steps down ahead of me." Jesus said to him, "Stand up, take your mat and walk." At once the man was made well, and he took up his mat and began to walk. Now that day was a sabbath. So the Jews said to the man who had been cured, "It is the sabbath; it is not lawful for you to carry your mat." But he answered them, "The man who made me well said to me, 'Take up your mat and walk.'" They asked him, "Who is the man who said to you, 'Take it up and walk'?" Now the man who had been healed did not know who it was, for Jesus had disappeared in the crowd that was there. Later Jesus found him in the temple and said to him, "See, you have been made well! Do not sin any more, so that nothing worse happens to you." The man went away and told the Jews that it was Jesus who had made him well. Therefore the Jews started persecuting Jesus, because he was doing such things on the sabbath.

- Thirty-eight years of waiting! Did Jesus single out this man, knowing that he had endured his illness longer than anyone else? Jesus speaks with him patiently and allows the man to reveal the pain of his isolation, but he also ignites his desire to be healed. Jesus tells us of his desire for the man: "Do not sin any more . . ."

- Are there sick people in your family, among your friends? Bring them one by one before the Lord, asking him to do what is best for them. Maybe you are worried about your own health? Tell the Lord of your anxieties and leave them with him. "Cast all your anxiety on him, because he cares for you" (1 Peter 5:7).

Wednesday 3rd April
John 5:17–30

[Jesus said,] "My Father is still working, and I also am working." For this reason the Jews were seeking all the more to kill him, because he was not only breaking the sabbath, but was also calling God his own Father, thereby making himself equal to God. Jesus said to them, "Very truly, I tell you, the Son can do nothing on his own, but only what he sees the Father doing; for whatever the Father does, the Son does likewise. The Father loves the Son and shows him all that he himself is doing; and he will show him greater works than these, so that you will be astonished. Indeed, just as the Father raises the dead and gives them life, so also the Son gives life to whomever he wishes. The Father judges no one but has given all judgment to the Son, so that all may honor the Son just as they honor the Father. Anyone who does not honor the Son does not honor the Father who sent him. Very truly, I tell you, anyone who hears my word and believes him who sent me has eternal life, and does not come under judgment, but has passed from death to life. Very truly, I tell you, the hour is coming, and is now here, when the dead will hear the voice of the Son of God, and those who hear will live. For just as the Father has life in himself, so he has granted the Son also to have life in himself; and he has given him authority to execute judgment, because he is the Son of Man. Do not be astonished at this; for the hour is coming when all who are in their graves will hear his voice and will come out—those who have done good, to the resurrection of life, and those who have done evil, to the resurrection of condemnation. I can do nothing on my own. As I hear, I judge; and my judgment is just, because I seek to do not my own will but the will of him who sent me."

- When John's Gospel speaks of "the Jews," it means those Jews who rejected Jesus; after all, Jesus and his disciples were Jews. When Jesus said that the Sabbath was made for man, and when he called God his Father, he was challenging his own people's vision of God, proclaiming that God is not so much a lawmaker as a loving father to all his children.

- "My Father is still working, and I also am working." St. Ignatius Loyola used to say that the Lord is ever laboring on our behalf: we receive an unexpected outcome, or we are in the right place at the right time. These are signs of God's providence at work. Thank the Lord for these moments.

Thursday 4th April

John 5:31–47

[Jesus said,] "If I testify about myself, my testimony is not true. There is another who testifies on my behalf, and I know that his testimony to me is true. You sent messengers to John, and he testified to the truth. Not that I accept such human testimony, but I say these things so that you may be saved. He was a burning and shining lamp, and you were willing to rejoice for a while in his light. But I have a testimony greater than John's. The works that the Father has given me to complete, the very works that I am doing, testify on my behalf that the Father has sent me. And the Father who sent me has himself testified on my behalf. You have never heard his voice or seen his form, and you do not have his word abiding in you, because you do not believe him whom he has sent. You search the scriptures because you think that in them you have eternal life; and it is they that testify on my behalf. Yet you refuse to come to me to have life. I do not accept glory from human beings. But I know that you do not have the love of God in you. I have come in my Father's name, and you do not accept me; if another comes in his own name, you will accept him. How can you believe when you accept glory from one another and do not seek the glory that comes from the one who alone is God? Do not think that I will accuse you before the Father; your accuser is Moses, on whom you have set your hope. If you believed Moses, you would believe me, for he wrote about me. But if you do not believe what he wrote, how will you believe what I say?"

- This is a difficult text. However, praying is not study. Focus on what you understand! Jesus is ever aware of having been sent by his Father. The only approval that matters is his Father's, which he received at his baptism and transfiguration. "This is my Son, the Beloved, with whom I am well pleased" (Matthew 3:17; 17:5). While Jesus has the freedom to speak of the Father and his kingdom despite opposition, he is, like us, sensitive to ridicule and hostility.

- Thank the Lord for the encouragement that came from home, school, and friends. Seek to forgive those who were a source of discouragement.

Friday 5th April
John 7:1–2, 10, 25–30

Jesus went about in Galilee. He did not wish to go about in Judea because the Jews were looking for an opportunity to kill him. Now the Jewish festival of Booths was near. . . . But after his brothers had gone to the festival, then he also went, not publicly but as it were in secret. . . . Now some of the people of

Jerusalem were saying, "Is not this the man whom they are trying to kill? And here he is, speaking openly, but they say nothing to him! Can it be that the authorities really know that this is the Messiah? Yet we know where this man is from; but when the Messiah comes, no one will know where he is from." Then Jesus cried out as he was teaching in the temple, "You know me, and you know where I am from. I have not come on my own. But the one who sent me is true, and you do not know him. I know him, because I am from him, and he sent me." Then they tried to arrest him, but no one laid hands on him, because his hour had not yet come.

- Notice "as it were in secret." Jesus never made himself the center. He was ever pointing to his Father and, toward the end of his life, speaking of the Spirit who was to come. "They tried to arrest him . . ." On the horizon was the day when "his hour" would come, the hour of his death, the hour of his glory. "Having loved his own who were in the world, he loved them to the end." (John 13:1)

- Bow in silence before the mystery that is God: Father, Son, and Holy Spirit, and pray slowly, "Glory be to the Father and to the Son and to the Holy Spirit."

Saturday 6th April

John 7:40–53

When they heard these words, some in the crowd said, "This is really the prophet." Others said, "This is the Messiah." But some asked, "Surely the Messiah does not come from Galilee, does he? Has not the scripture said that the Messiah is descended from David and comes from Bethlehem, the village where David lived?" So there was a division in the crowd because of him. Some of them wanted to arrest him, but no one laid hands on him. Then the temple police went back to the chief priests and Pharisees, who asked them, "Why did you not arrest him?" The police answered, "Never has anyone spoken like this!" Then the Pharisees replied, "Surely you have not been deceived too, have you? Has any one of the authorities or of the Pharisees believed in him? But this crowd, which does not know the law—they are accursed." Nicodemus, who had gone to Jesus before, and who was one of them, asked, "Our law does not judge people without first giving them a hearing to find out what they are doing, does it?" They replied, "Surely you are not also from Galilee, are you? Search and you will see that no prophet is to arise from Galilee." Then each of them went home.

- Here are two ways of approaching Jesus: some hear him, see how he lives, and love and enjoy him.

Others go back to their books and argue about his pedigree. Lord, save me from losing you in the babble of books and arguments. May I meet and know and enjoy you.

- "Never has anyone spoken like this!" I can hear Jesus speak to me from the Scriptures anytime I want—but perhaps the words have been dulled through familiarity? I ask the Holy Spirit to help me regain my sense of wonder at the newness of God.

April 7—April 13

Something to think and pray about each day this week:

People ask me all the time, "How do I know if I'm hearing God's voice or not?" While I don't have the million-dollar answer to this question, I *can* tell you this: A way to recognize God's voice is to spend time praying with Scripture. Scripture is truly the word of God and voice of God. If we want to tune our ear to God's voice, why not start with what we know is God's word? Think about it this way. In a room of young children, I distinctly know when one of my own children is calling out, "Mom!" or when it's another child. Why? Because I've spent hours and hours and hours listening to my children's voices. My ear is finely attuned to what their voices sound like. I can also typically discern which of my children is calling me. I do not think about this anymore; it's just something that naturally happens in motherhood— training our ear to our children's voices. In the same way, as we continue to meditate on God's word, we become more and more attuned to what God's voice sounds like to us.

—Becky Eldredge, *Busy Lives & Restless Souls*

The Presence of God

Dear Jesus, today I call on you, but not to ask for anything. I'd like only to dwell in your presence. May my heart respond to your love.

Freedom

God my creator, you gave me life and the gift of freedom. Through your love I exist in this world. May I never take the gift of life for granted. May I always respect others' right to life.

Consciousness

I ask how I am today. Am I particularly tired, stressed, or anxious? If any of these characteristics apply, can I try to let go of the concerns that disturb me?

The Word

The word of God comes down to us through the Scriptures. May the Holy Spirit enlighten my mind and my heart to respond to the gospel teachings. (Please turn to the Scripture on the following pages. Inspiration points are there, should you need them. When you are ready, return here to continue.)

Conversation

I begin to talk with Jesus about the Scripture I have just read. What part of it strikes a chord in me? Perhaps the words of a friend—or some story I have heard recently—will rise to the surface in my consciousness. If so, does the story throw light on what the Scripture passage may be saying to me?

Conclusion

Glory be to the Father, and to the Son, and to the Holy Spirit,

As it was in the beginning, is now and ever shall be,

World without end. Amen.

Sunday 7th April

John 11:3–7, 17, 20–27, 33–45

So the sisters sent a message to Jesus, "Lord, he whom you love is ill." But when Jesus heard it, he said, "This illness does not lead to death; rather it is for God's glory, so that the Son of God may be glorified through it." Accordingly, though Jesus loved Martha and her sister and Lazarus, after having heard that Lazarus was ill, he stayed two days longer in the place where he was. Then after this he said to the disciples, "Let us go to Judea again." . . . When Jesus arrived, he found that Lazarus had already been in the tomb four days. . . . When Martha heard that Jesus was coming, she went and met him, while Mary stayed at home. Martha said to Jesus, "Lord, if you had been here, my brother would not have died. But even now I know that God will give you whatever you ask of him." Jesus said to her, "Your brother will rise again." Martha said to him, "I know that he will rise again in the resurrection on the last day." Jesus said to her, "I am the resurrection and the life. Those who believe in me, even though they die, will live, and everyone who lives and believes in me will never die. Do you believe this?" She said to him, "Yes, Lord, I believe that you are the Messiah, the Son of God, the one coming into the world." . . . When Jesus saw [Mary] weeping, and the Jews who came with her also weeping, he was greatly disturbed in spirit and deeply moved. He said, "Where have you laid him?" They said to him, "Lord, come and see." Jesus began to weep. So the Jews said, "See how he loved him!" But some of them said, "Could not he who opened the eyes of the blind man have kept this man from dying?" Then Jesus, again greatly disturbed, came to the tomb. It was a cave, and a stone was lying against it. Jesus said, "Take away the stone." Martha, the sister of the dead man, said to him, "Lord, already there is a stench because he has been dead four days." Jesus said to her, "Did I not tell you that if you believed, you would see the glory of God?" So they took away the stone. And Jesus looked upward and said, "Father, I thank you for having heard me. I knew that you always hear me, but I have said this for the sake of the crowd standing here, so that they may believe that you sent me." When he had said this, he cried with a loud voice, "Lazarus, come out!" The dead man came out, his hands and feet bound with strips of cloth, and his face wrapped in a cloth. Jesus said to them, "Unbind him, and let him go." Many of the Jews therefore, who had come with Mary and had seen what Jesus did, believed in him.

- Jesus reminds us many times that, if we have faith, nothing is impossible. Martha's faith is indomitable. Knowing that the tomb contains the decomposing body of her beloved brother, she can still summon up the words, "even now I know that God will give you whatever you ask of him." Do I truly believe that anything is possible for one who believes?

• When I am entombed in hopelessness, grant that I may hear the voice of Jesus, as Lazarus did. Let me hear those blessed words he uttered at Lazarus's grave: "Unbind him, and let him go."

Monday 8th April
John 8:12–20

Again Jesus spoke to them, saying, "I am the light of the world. Whoever follows me will never walk in darkness but will have the light of life." Then the Pharisees said to him, "You are testifying on your own behalf; your testimony is not valid." Jesus answered, "Even if I testify on my own behalf, my testimony is valid because I know where I have come from and where I am going, but you do not know where I come from or where I am going. You judge by human standards; I judge no one. Yet even if I do judge, my judgment is valid; for it is not I alone who judge, but I and the Father who sent me. In your law it is written that the testimony of two witnesses is valid. I testify on my own behalf, and the Father who sent me testifies on my behalf." Then they said to him, "Where is your Father?" Jesus answered, "You know neither me nor my Father. If you knew me, you would know my Father also." He spoke these words while he was teaching in the treasury of the temple, but no one arrested him, because his hour had not yet come.

- We revisit the question of Jesus' identity. The passage begins with one of the "I am" sayings that John attributes to Jesus. These are meant to recall the answer God gave to Moses when he asked God's name: "I AM WHO I AM." Then Moses is told to say to the Israelites: "I AM has sent me to you" (Exodus 3:13–14). Jesus, by using this "I am" language, is claiming to share in God's own identity.

- Christian faith is not primarily in a doctrine but in a person. Through this person, Jesus Christ, we enter the mystery of God. Thank you, Lord, for welcoming me.

Tuesday 9th April
John 8:21–30

Again he said to them, "I am going away, and you will search for me, but you will die in your sin. Where I am going, you cannot come." Then the Jews said, "Is he going to kill himself? Is that what he means by saying, 'Where I am going, you cannot come'?"

He said to them, "You are from below, I am from above; you are of this world, I am not of this world. I told you that you would die in your sins, for you will die in your sins unless you believe that I am he." They said to him, "Who are you?" Jesus said to them, "Why do I speak to you at all? I have much to say about you and much to condemn; but the one who sent me is true, and I declare to the world what I have heard from him." They did not understand that he was speaking to them about the Father. So Jesus said, "When you have lifted up the Son of Man, then you will realize that I am he, and that I do nothing on my own, but I speak these things as the Father instructed me. And the one who sent me is with me; he has not left me alone, for I always do what is pleasing to him." As he was saying these things, many believed in him.

- It is when we see Jesus lifted up on the cross that we realize who he is and why he lived. The rest of the Gospels are like a preface to the Passion. On the cross we see the triumph of love over evil, and our best help in coping with the reality of evil.

- Jesus spoke to the world what he heard from the Father. Am I aware, day to day, that I can listen for God's voice and then repeat to others what I hear? Am I that confident in my relationship with the Father? Father, help me settle into my role as son or daughter with comfort, hope, and courage.

Wednesday 10th April

John 8:31–42

Then Jesus said to the Jews who had believed in him, "If you continue in my word, you are truly my disciples; and you will know the truth, and the truth will make you free." They answered him, "We are descendants of Abraham and have never been slaves to anyone. What do you mean by saying, 'You will be made free'?" Jesus answered them, "Very truly, I tell you, everyone who commits sin is a slave to sin. The slave does not have a permanent place in the household; the son has a place there forever. So if the Son makes you free, you will be free indeed. I know that you are descendants of Abraham; yet you look for an opportunity to kill me, because there is no place in you for my word. I declare what I have seen in the Father's presence; as for you, you should do what you have heard from the Father." They answered him, "Abraham is our father." Jesus said to them, "If you were Abraham's children, you would be doing what Abraham did, but now you are trying to kill me, a man who has told you the truth that I heard from God. This is not what Abraham did. You are indeed doing what your father does." They said to him, "We are not illegitimate children; we have one father, God himself." Jesus said to them, "If God were your Father, you would love me, for I came from

God and now I am here. I did not come on my own, but he sent me."

- Jesus' promise is that the truth will make us free. Lord, I do want to be free, so let me listen to those who tell me the truth about myself. Let me listen also to your word, which reaches into my heart to liberate me. Let me start with the great truth of which you try to convince me: I am endlessly loved by you.

- When in my life have I had an experience that made me truly see Jesus as the one sent by God?

Thursday 11th April
John 8:51–59

[Jesus said,] "Very truly, I tell you, whoever keeps my word will never see death." The Jews said to him, "Now we know that you have a demon. Abraham died, and so did the prophets; yet you say, 'Whoever keeps my word will never taste death.' Are you greater than our father Abraham, who died? The prophets also died. Who do you claim to be?" Jesus answered, "If I glorify myself, my glory is nothing. It is my Father who glorifies me, he of whom you say, 'He is our God,' though you do not know him. But I know him; if I were to say that I do not know him, I would be a liar like you. But I do know him and I keep his word. Your ancestor Abraham rejoiced that he would see my day; he saw it and was glad." Then the Jews said to him, "You are not yet fifty years old, and have you seen Abraham?" Jesus said to them, "Very truly, I tell you, before Abraham was, I am." So they picked up stones to throw at him, but Jesus hid himself and went out of the temple.

- Lord, I am praying here on the edge of what I can grasp, reaching for the eternal Now. What matters to me is that you are as much my contemporary as you were of Pilate and the stone-throwing Jews.

- Abraham's life marks the beginning of salvation history. His immense journey through the wilderness was made in response to God's call. The biblical desert was a place of passage and purification. In our own passage to the Promised Land, we must learn that God is with us at every stage of the journey, as he was with Abraham.

Friday 12th April
John 10:31–42

The Jews took up stones again to stone him. Jesus replied, "I have shown you many good works from the Father. For which of these are you going to stone me?" The Jews answered, "It is not for a good work that we are going to stone you, but for blasphemy, because you, though only a human being, are making yourself God." Jesus answered, "Is it not written in your law, 'I said, you are gods'? If those to whom the word of God came were called 'gods'—and the scripture cannot be annulled—can you say that the one whom the Father has sanctified and sent into the world is blaspheming because I said, 'I am God's Son'? If I am not doing the works of my Father, then do not believe me. But if I do them, even though you do not believe me, believe the works, so that you may know and understand that the Father is in me and I am in the Father." Then they tried to arrest him again, but he escaped from their hands. He went away again across the Jordan to the place where John had been baptizing earlier, and he remained there. Many came to him, and they were saying, "John performed no sign, but everything that John said about this man was true." And many believed in him there.

- Lord, you told the Jews to look at your works, if they did not believe your words. Compassion, kindness, and courage in my life are what make my words credible. May my life reflect what I profess.

- The people in today's reading condemn Jesus because of their particular image of God. What is my image of God? The best image is to see God as Pure Love. Have I ever condemned someone because I nursed a warped image of God?

Saturday 13th April

John 11:45–56

Many of the Jews therefore, who had come with
Mary and had seen what Jesus did, believed in him.
But some of them went to the Pharisees and told
them what he had done. So the chief priests and the
Pharisees called a meeting of the council, and said,
"What are we to do? This man is performing many
signs. If we let him go on like this, everyone will believe in him, and the Romans will come and destroy
both our holy place and our nation." But one of them,
Caiaphas, who was high priest that year, said to them,
"You know nothing at all! You do not understand
that it is better for you to have one man die for the
people than to have the whole nation destroyed." He
did not say this on his own, but being high priest that
year he prophesied that Jesus was about to die for the
nation, and not for the nation only, but to gather into
one the dispersed children of God. So from that day
on they planned to put him to death. Jesus therefore
no longer walked about openly among the Jews, but
went from there to a town called Ephraim in the re-
gion near the wilderness; and he remained there with
the disciples. Now the Passover of the Jews was near,
and many went up from the country to Jerusalem
before the Passover to purify themselves. They were
looking for Jesus and were asking one another as they

stood in the temple, "What do you think? Surely he will not come to the festival, will he?"

- Pope Francis, reflecting on this text, noted that Jesus died for his people and for everyone. But this, the Pope stressed, must not be applied generically; it means that Jesus died specifically for each and every one of us individually. And this is the ultimate expression of Jesus' love for all people.

- The religious leaders were caught up in the politics of the day, which included dealing with the Roman occupiers. From a political standpoint, Caiaphas's conclusion made sense. How do politics or other details in my life press upon the way I make decisions or discern my next steps?

Holy Week
April 14—April 20

Something to think and pray about each day this week:

We kneel before a crucifix and recall that death, a consequence of sin, has no power over Jesus of Nazareth. He hangs on a cross embracing death. At the end, *crying out in a loud voice*, Jesus deliberately *yielded up his spirit* (Matt. 27:50, NJB). What can we believe about this faith handed on to us, so utterly contradictory to the human instincts and our sophisticated culture? We can believe that we contemplate a love so entire that the Son would want to embrace everything human—even suffering and death. We know what the faith teaches us: Jesus "sacrificed his life" for love of us. We struggle, though, to believe in a love so entire that it remains faithful when not returned. Unreturned love is a profound form of suffering. And Jesus' unreturned love was not just not returned; it was violently, disdainfully rejected. No one will understand so great a love who has not experienced it. God knows that is true. He knew it about his own people. So God sent the Son to show us that love, and Jesus did so, publicly suffering rejection and execution. Then he invited us to *love one another as I have loved you* (John 15:12).

—Joseph A. Tetlow, SJ, *Always Discerning*

The Presence of God
God is with me, but even more astounding, God is within me.
Let me dwell for a moment on God's life-giving presence
in my body, in my mind, in my heart,
as I sit here, right now.

Freedom
Lord, may I never take the gift of freedom for granted. You gave me the great blessing of freedom of spirit. Fill my spirit with your peace and joy.

Consciousness
I remind myself that I am in the presence of God, who is my strength in times of weakness and my comforter in times of sorrow.

The Word
I take my time to read the word of God slowly, a few times, allowing myself to dwell on anything that strikes me. (Please turn to the Scripture on the following pages. Inspiration points are there, should you need them. When you are ready, return here to continue.)

Conversation
Jesus, you always welcomed little children when you walked on this earth. Teach me to have a childlike trust in you. Teach me to live in the knowledge that you will never abandon me.

Conclusion
Glory be to the Father, and to the Son, and to the Holy Spirit,
As it was in the beginning, is now and ever shall be,
World without end. Amen.

Sunday 14th April
Palm Sunday of the Passion of the Lord
Luke 23:1–49

Then the assembly rose as a body and brought Jesus before Pilate. They began to accuse him, saying, "We found this man perverting our nation, forbidding us to pay taxes to the emperor, and saying that he himself is the Messiah, a king." Then Pilate asked him, "Are you the king of the Jews?" He answered, "You say so." Then Pilate said to the chief priests and the crowds, "I find no basis for an accusation against this man." But they were insistent and said, "He stirs up the people by teaching throughout all Judea, from Galilee where he began even to this place."

When Pilate heard this, he asked whether the man was a Galilean. And when he learned that he was under Herod's jurisdiction, he sent him off to Herod, who was himself in Jerusalem at that time. When Herod saw Jesus, he was very glad, for he had been wanting to see him for a long time, because he had heard about him and was hoping to see him perform some sign. He questioned him at some length, but Jesus gave him no answer. The chief priests and the scribes stood by, vehemently accusing him. Even Herod with his soldiers treated him with contempt and mocked him; then he put an elegant robe on him, and sent him back to Pilate. That same day

Herod and Pilate became friends with each other; before this they had been enemies.

Pilate then called together the chief priests, the leaders, and the people, and said to them, "You brought me this man as one who was perverting the people; and here I have examined him in your presence and have not found this man guilty of any of your charges against him. Neither has Herod, for he sent him back to us. Indeed, he has done nothing to deserve death. I will therefore have him flogged and release him."

Then they all shouted out together, "Away with this fellow! Release Barabbas for us!" (This was a man who had been put in prison for an insurrection that had taken place in the city, and for murder.) Pilate, wanting to release Jesus, addressed them again; but they kept shouting, "Crucify, crucify him!" A third time he said to them, "Why, what evil has he done? I have found in him no ground for the sentence of death; I will therefore have him flogged and then release him." But they kept urgently demanding with loud shouts that he should be crucified; and their voices prevailed. So Pilate gave his verdict that their demand should be granted. He released the man they asked for, the one who had been put in prison for insurrection and murder, and he handed Jesus over as they wished.

As they led him away, they seized a man, Simon of Cyrene, who was coming from the country, and they laid the cross on him, and made him carry it behind Jesus. A great number of the people followed him, and among them were women who were beating their breasts and wailing for him. But Jesus turned to them and said, "Daughters of Jerusalem, do not weep for me, but weep for yourselves and for your children. For the days are surely coming when they will say, 'Blessed are the barren, and the wombs that never bore, and the breasts that never nursed.' Then they will begin to say to the mountains, 'Fall on us'; and to the hills, 'Cover us.' For if they do this when the wood is green, what will happen when it is dry?"

Two others also, who were criminals, were led away to be put to death with him. When they came to the place that is called The Skull, they crucified Jesus there with the criminals, one on his right and one on his left. Then Jesus said, "Father, forgive them; for they do not know what they are doing." And they cast lots to divide his clothing. And the people stood by, watching; but the leaders scoffed at him, saying, "He saved others; let him save himself if he is the Messiah of God, his chosen one!" The soldiers also mocked him, coming up and offering him sour wine, and saying, "If you are the King of the Jews, save yourself!" There was also an inscription over him, "This is the King of the Jews."

One of the criminals who were hanged there kept deriding him and saying, "Are you not the Messiah? Save yourself and us!" But the other rebuked him, saying, "Do you not fear God, since you are under the same sentence of condemnation? And we indeed have been condemned justly, for we are getting what we deserve for our deeds, but this man has done nothing wrong." Then he said, "Jesus, remember me when you come into your kingdom." He replied, "Truly I tell you, today you will be with me in Paradise."

It was now about noon, and darkness came over the whole land until three in the afternoon, while the sun's light failed; and the curtain of the temple was torn in two. Then Jesus, crying with a loud voice, said, "Father, into your hands I commend my spirit." Having said this, he breathed his last. When the centurion saw what had taken place, he praised God and said, "Certainly this man was innocent." And when all the crowds who had gathered there for this spectacle saw what had taken place, they returned home, beating their breasts. But all his acquaintances, including the women who had followed him from Galilee, stood at a distance, watching these things.

- I choose a moment or a scene from this long story of Jesus' Passion, and I stay with Jesus. I tell him how I feel about what is happening. I try to comfort him.

- Lord Jesus, show me how to be present to people who are suffering—people I know who are being persecuted or mistreated or misunderstood and ostracized.

Monday 15th April
John 12:1–11

Six days before the Passover Jesus came to Bethany, the home of Lazarus, whom he had raised from the dead. There they gave a dinner for him. Martha served, and Lazarus was one of those at the table with him. Mary took a pound of costly perfume made of pure nard, anointed Jesus' feet, and wiped them with her hair. The house was filled with the fragrance of the perfume. But Judas Iscariot, one of his disciples (the one who was about to betray him), said, "Why was this perfume not sold for three hundred denarii and the money given to the poor?" (He said this not because he cared about the poor, but because he was a thief; he kept the common purse and used to steal what was put into it.) Jesus said, "Leave her alone. She bought it so that she might keep it for the day of my burial. You always have the poor with you, but you do not always have me." When the great crowd of the Jews learned that he was there, they came not only because of Jesus but also to see Lazarus, whom he had raised from the dead. So the chief priests planned to put Lazarus to death as well, since it was on account of him that many of the Jews were deserting and were believing in Jesus.

- Where Judas sees waste, Jesus sees love. Mary's love anticipates the love of Jesus. She pours her tears on the feet of the one who will pour himself out on the world. Lord, may I honor the vision and wisdom you have given me to understand events with my deepest self.

- Mary is praying with her body and with her heart. It is a way we seldom pray. Her prayer is part of a tradition as old as the passionate, lyrical, and sensuous Song of Solomon. Yet there is nothing to stop us praying this way. A gentle touch of understanding, a hug of reassurance, a smile of love—these, too, are prayers.

Tuesday 16th April
John 13:21–33, 36–38

After saying this Jesus was troubled in spirit, and declared, "Very truly, I tell you, one of you will betray me." The disciples looked at one another, uncertain of whom he was speaking. One of his disciples—the one whom Jesus loved—was reclining next to him; Simon Peter therefore motioned to him to ask Jesus of whom he was speaking. So while reclining next to Jesus, he asked him, "Lord, who is it?" Jesus answered, "It is the one to whom I give this piece of bread when I have dipped it in the dish." So when he had dipped the piece of bread, he gave it to Judas son of Simon Iscariot. After he received the piece of bread, Satan entered into him. Jesus said to him, "Do quickly what you are going to do." Now no one at the table knew why he said this to him. Some thought that, because Judas had the common purse, Jesus was telling him, "Buy what we need for the festival"; or, that he should give something to the poor. So, after receiving the piece of bread, he immediately went out. And it was night. When he had gone out, Jesus said, "Now the Son of Man has been glorified, and God has been glorified in him. If God has been glorified in him, God will also glorify him in himself and will glorify him at once. Little children, I am with you only a little longer. You will look for me; and as I said to the Jews so now I say to you, 'Where I am going, you cannot come.'" . . . Simon Peter said to him, "Lord, where are you going?" Jesus answered, "Where I am going, you cannot follow me now; but you will follow afterward." Peter said to him, "Lord, why can I not follow you now? I will lay down my life for you." Jesus answered, "Will you lay down your life for me? Very truly, I tell you, before the cock crows, you will have denied me three times."

- "And it was night" is not simply a description of the time of day; it is a stark image of the gloom of sin and rejection. Judas walks into the darkness— away from Jesus, the true light that the darkness cannot overcome. He will die in despair, in a pride so stiff-necked that it selects the misery of damnation rather than the happiness offered by a kindly God.

- Peter hit deep points of his life here. His sureness of following Jesus was challenged by Jesus himself. He would later find himself weak and failing. But even when Peter said later that he didn't know Jesus, there would be time for taking it back and speaking it with his life. We oscillate in our following of the Lord; these days let us know in the certainty of Jesus' love that there is always another day, another chance, another joy in our following of Jesus.

Wednesday 17th April

Matthew 26:14–25

Then one of the twelve, who was called Judas Iscariot, went to the chief priests and said, "What will you give me if I betray him to you?" They paid him thirty pieces of silver. And from that moment he began to look for an opportunity to betray him. On the first day of Unleavened Bread the disciples came to Jesus, saying, "Where do you want us to make the preparations for you to eat the Passover?" He said, "Go into the city to a certain man, and say to him, 'The Teacher says, My time is near; I will keep the Passover at your house with my disciples.'" So the disciples did as Jesus had directed them, and they prepared the Passover meal. When it was evening, he took his place with the twelve; and while they were eating, he said, "Truly I tell you, one of you will betray me." And they became greatly distressed and began to say to him one after another, "Surely not I, Lord?" He answered, "The one who has dipped his hand into the bowl with me will betray me. The Son of Man goes as it is written of him, but woe to that one by whom the Son of Man is betrayed! It would have been better for that one not to have been born." Judas, who betrayed him, said, "Surely not I, Rabbi?" He replied, "You have said so."

• Holy Week is an invitation to walk closely with Jesus: we fix our gaze on him and accompany him in his suffering; we let him look closely at us and see us as we really are. We do not have to present a brave face to him but can tell him about where we have been disappointed, let down, perhaps even betrayed. We avoid getting stuck in our own misfortune by seeing as he sees, by learning from his heart.

• Help me to see, Jesus, how you do not condemn. You invite each of us to embrace the truth of our own discipleship. You invite us to follow you willingly, freely, forgiven.

Thursday 18th April
Holy Thursday
John 13:1–15

Now before the festival of the Passover, Jesus knew that his hour had come to depart from this world and go to the Father. Having loved his own who were in the world, he loved them to the end. The devil had already put it into the heart of Judas son of Simon Iscariot to betray him. And during supper Jesus, knowing that the Father had given all things into his hands, and that he had come from God and was going to God, got up from the table, took off his outer robe, and tied a towel around himself. Then he poured water into a basin and began to wash the disciples' feet and to wipe them with the towel that was tied around him. He came to Simon Peter, who said to him, "Lord, are you going to wash my feet?" Jesus answered, "You do not know now what I am doing, but later you will understand." Peter said to him, "You will never wash my feet." Jesus answered, "Unless I wash you, you have no share with me." Simon Peter said to him, "Lord, not my feet only but also my hands and my head!" Jesus said to him, "One who has bathed does not need to wash, except for the feet, but is entirely clean. And you are clean, though not all of you." For he knew who was to betray him; for this reason he said, "Not all of you are clean." After he had washed their feet, had put on his robe, and had returned to the table, he said to them, "Do you know what I have done to you? You call me Teacher and Lord—and you are right, for that is what I am. So if I, your Lord and Teacher, have washed your feet, you also ought to wash one another's feet. For I have set you an example, that you also should do as I have done to you."

- It may be important for us to think of what we want to do for Jesus, to let him know and to seek his approval. Jesus smiles and invites us to listen first—to notice. He asks if we can allow him to serve us. "See what I do," he seems to say. "Accept who I am. Then be who you are!"

- Jesus says, "Later you will understand." Sometimes that's not enough for me! I want to understand now. Help me, Jesus, to live as you did even when I don't fully comprehend what you are asking of me.

Friday 19th April
Friday of the Passion of the Lord
(Good Friday)

John 18:1—19:42

After Jesus had spoken these words, he went out with his disciples across the Kidron valley to a place where there was a garden, which he and his disciples entered. Now Judas, who betrayed him, also knew the place, because Jesus often met there with his disciples. So Judas brought a detachment of soldiers together with police from the chief priests and the Pharisees, and they came there with lanterns and torches and weapons. Then Jesus, knowing all that was to happen to him, came forward and asked them, "Whom are you looking for?" They answered, "Jesus of Nazareth." Jesus replied, "I am he." Judas, who betrayed him, was standing with them. When Jesus said to them, "I am he," they stepped back and fell to the ground. Again he asked them, "Whom are you looking for?" And they said, "Jesus of Nazareth." Jesus answered, "I told you that I am he. So if you are looking for me, let these men go." This was to fulfill the word that he had spoken, "I did not lose a single one of those whom you gave me." Then Simon Peter, who had a sword, drew it, struck the high priest's slave, and cut off his right ear. The slave's name was Malchus. Jesus said to Peter, "Put your sword back into its sheath.

Am I not to drink the cup that the Father has given me?"

So the soldiers, their officer, and the Jewish police arrested Jesus and bound him. First they took him to Annas, who was the father-in-law of Caiaphas, the high priest that year. Caiaphas was the one who had advised the Jews that it was better to have one person die for the people.

Simon Peter and another disciple followed Jesus. Since that disciple was known to the high priest, he went with Jesus into the courtyard of the high priest, but Peter was standing outside at the gate. So the other disciple, who was known to the high priest, went out, spoke to the woman who guarded the gate, and brought Peter in. The woman said to Peter, "You are not also one of this man's disciples, are you?" He said, "I am not." Now the slaves and the police had made a charcoal fire because it was cold, and they were standing around it and warming themselves. Peter also was standing with them and warming himself.

Then the high priest questioned Jesus about his disciples and about his teaching. Jesus answered, "I have spoken openly to the world; I have always taught in synagogues and in the temple, where all the Jews come together. I have said nothing in secret. Why do you ask me? Ask those who heard what I said to them; they know what I said." When he had said this, one of the police standing nearby struck Jesus on the face, saying, "Is that how you answer the high priest?" Jesus answered, "If I have spoken wrongly, testify to the wrong. But if I have spoken rightly, why do you strike me?" Then Annas sent him bound to Caiaphas the high priest.

Now Simon Peter was standing and warming himself. They asked him, "You are not also one of his disciples, are you?" He denied it and said, "I am not." One of the slaves of the high priest, a relative of the man whose ear Peter had cut off, asked, "Did I not see you in the garden with him?" Again Peter denied it, and at that moment the cock crowed.

Then they took Jesus from Caiaphas to Pilate's headquarters. It was early in the morning. They themselves did not enter the headquarters, so as to avoid ritual defilement and to be able to eat the Passover. So Pilate went out to them and said, "What accusation do you bring against this man?" They answered, "If this man were not a criminal, we would not have handed him over to you." Pilate said to them, "Take him yourselves and judge him according to your law." The Jews replied, "We are not permitted to put anyone to death." (This was to fulfill what Jesus had said when he indicated the kind of death he was to die.)

Then Pilate entered the headquarters again, summoned Jesus, and asked him, "Are you the King of the Jews?" Jesus answered, "Do you ask this on your own, or did others tell you about me?" Pilate replied,

"I am not a Jew, am I? Your own nation and the chief priests have handed you over to me. What have you done?" Jesus answered, "My kingdom is not from this world. If my kingdom were from this world, my followers would be fighting to keep me from being handed over to the Jews. But as it is, my kingdom is not from here." Pilate asked him, "So you are a king?" Jesus answered, "You say that I am a king. For this I was born, and for this I came into the world, to testify to the truth. Everyone who belongs to the truth listens to my voice." Pilate asked him, "What is truth?"

After he had said this, he went out to the Jews again and told them, "I find no case against him. But you have a custom that I release someone for you at the Passover. Do you want me to release for you the King of the Jews?" They shouted in reply, "Not this man, but Barabbas!" Now Barabbas was a bandit.

Then Pilate took Jesus and had him flogged. And the soldiers wove a crown of thorns and put it on his head, and they dressed him in a purple robe. They kept coming up to him, saying, "Hail, King of the Jews!" and striking him on the face. Pilate went out again and said to them, "Look, I am bringing him out to you to let you know that I find no case against him." So Jesus came out, wearing the crown of thorns and the purple robe. Pilate said to them, "Here is the man!" When the chief priests and the police saw him, they shouted, "Crucify him! Crucify him!" Pilate said to them, "Take him yourselves and crucify him; I find no case against him." The Jews answered him, "We have a law, and according to that law he ought to die because he has claimed to be the Son of God."

Now when Pilate heard this, he was more afraid than ever. He entered his headquarters again and asked Jesus, "Where are you from?" But Jesus gave him no answer. Pilate therefore said to him, "Do you refuse to speak to me? Do you not know that I have power to release you, and power to crucify you?" Jesus answered him, "You would have no power over me unless it had been given you from above; therefore the one who handed me over to you is guilty of a greater sin." From then on Pilate tried to release him, but the Jews cried out, "If you release this man, you are no friend of the emperor. Everyone who claims to be a king sets himself against the emperor."

When Pilate heard these words, he brought Jesus outside and sat on the judge's bench at a place called The Stone Pavement, or in Hebrew Gabbatha. Now it was the day of Preparation for the Passover; and it was about noon. He said to the Jews, "Here is your King!" They cried out, "Away with him! Away with him! Crucify him!" Pilate asked them, "Shall I crucify your King?" The chief priests answered, "We have no king but the emperor." Then he handed him over to them to be crucified.

So they took Jesus; and carrying the cross by himself, he went out to what is called The Place of the Skull, which in Hebrew is called Golgotha. There they crucified him, and with him two others, one on either side, with Jesus between them. Pilate also had an inscription written and put on the cross. It read, "Jesus of Nazareth, the King of the Jews." Many of the Jews read this inscription, because the place where Jesus was crucified was near the city; and it was written in Hebrew, in Latin, and in Greek. Then the chief priests of the Jews said to Pilate, "Do not write, 'The King of the Jews,' but, 'This man said, I am King of the Jews.'" Pilate answered, "What I have written I have written." When the soldiers had crucified Jesus, they took his clothes and divided them into four parts, one for each soldier. They also took his tunic; now the tunic was seamless, woven in one piece from the top. So they said to one another, "Let us not tear it, but cast lots for it to see who will get it." This was to fulfill what the scripture says, "They divided my clothes among themselves, and for my clothing they cast lots." And that is what the soldiers did.

Meanwhile, standing near the cross of Jesus were his mother, and his mother's sister, Mary the wife of Clopas, and Mary Magdalene. When Jesus saw his mother and the disciple whom he loved standing beside her, he said to his mother, "Woman, here is your son." Then he said to the disciple, "Here is your mother." And from that hour the disciple took her into his own home.

After this, when Jesus knew that all was now finished, he said (in order to fulfill the scripture), "I am thirsty." A jar full of sour wine was standing there. So they put a sponge full of the wine on a branch of hyssop and held it to his mouth. When Jesus had received the wine, he said, "It is finished." Then he bowed his head and gave up his spirit.

Since it was the day of Preparation, the Jews did not want the bodies left on the cross during the sabbath, especially because that sabbath was a day of great solemnity. So they asked Pilate to have the legs of the crucified men broken and the bodies removed. Then the soldiers came and broke the legs of the first and of the other who had been crucified with him. But when they came to Jesus and saw that he was already dead, they did not break his legs. Instead, one of the soldiers pierced his side with a spear, and at once blood and water came out. (He who saw this has testified so that you also may believe. His testimony is true, and he knows that he tells the truth.) These things occurred so that the scripture might be fulfilled, "None of his bones shall be broken." And again another passage of scripture says, "They will look on the one whom they have pierced."

After these things, Joseph of Arimathea, who was a disciple of Jesus, though a secret one because of his fear of the Jews, asked Pilate to let him take away the body of Jesus. Pilate gave him permission; so he came and removed his body. Nicodemus, who had at first come to Jesus by night, also came, bringing a mixture of myrrh and aloes, weighing about a hundred pounds. They took the body of Jesus and wrapped it with the spices in linen cloths, according to the burial custom of the Jews. Now there was a garden in the place where he was crucified, and in the garden there was a new tomb in which no one had ever been laid. And so, because it was the Jewish day of Preparation, and the tomb was nearby, they laid Jesus there.

- Jesus allows himself to be caught up in a sequence of events fueled by hatred, racism (Romans against Jews), pride, fear, and political expediency. He does not use his power to change anyone's mind or will. Lord, help me give myself to this day of my own life, willing to be who I am in you and yet not striving to force change in others.

- Linger with Jesus at any point in this sequence of events. Watch his face and body, say what you long to say to him.

Saturday 20th April
Holy Saturday

Luke 24:1–12

But on the first day of the week, at early dawn, they came to the tomb, taking the spices that they had prepared. They found the stone rolled away from the tomb, but when they went in, they did not find the body. While they were perplexed about this, suddenly two men in dazzling clothes stood beside them. The women were terrified and bowed their faces to the ground, but the men said to them, "Why do you look for the living among the dead? He is not here, but has risen. Remember how he told you, while he was still in Galilee, that the Son of Man must be handed over to sinners, and be crucified, and on the third day rise again." Then they remembered his words, and returning from the tomb, they told all this to the eleven and to all the rest. Now it was Mary Magdalene, Joanna, Mary the mother of James, and the other women with them who told this to the apostles. But these words seemed to them an idle tale, and they did not believe them. But Peter got up and ran to the tomb; stooping and looking in, he saw the linen cloths by themselves; then he went home, amazed at what had happened.

- Holy Saturday is a day of waiting for what is to come (whatever that may be). The emptiness in our hearts left by the death of a loved one is mirrored by the emptiness of the tomb. Not only do we no longer have a living Jesus, neither do we have his dead body. It is the women disciples who first hear the news that Jesus is risen. But this only throws them into greater confusion, as they cannot understand what it might mean, and the apostles think their whole story is "an idle tale." What would my response be to what the women say?

• Yet Peter, impulsive as ever, and still feeling overwhelmed by guilt because of his denial of Jesus, runs to the tomb to check out the story. He too finds it empty. What does that empty tomb say to me?

April 21

Something to think and pray about today:

The sun is up now, and you look up to feel the warmth of the rays against your face. Looking ahead, you notice some women running down the path. They seem to be in a joyful panic, like something frightening but wonderful has happened. As you get closer to where they came from, there is a man standing there. He is standing so tall, so confident. It's as if he has accomplished something impossible. Getting closer, you realize it's him. It's Jesus. You know you saw him die. How can he be standing there? He looks at you with eyes that are clear and sure. He speaks to you. What does Jesus say to you? How do you respond? Standing closer to Jesus, you feel a strength coming from him. You want to reach over and embrace him, to touch him to be sure it is really Jesus. He seems to know your mind and the questions swimming around in your head. Jesus reaches over and touches your hand. You feel a surge of energy rush through you. "It is you," you say to Jesus. "It is you!" Tears stream down your face. Jesus says something to you. What does Jesus say? What do you want to say to Jesus? . . . Easter Sunday is a day when life conquers death. How does my belief in the Resurrection change how I live my life? Who do I need to share the hope and joy of the Resurrection with today?

—Steve Connor on *dotMagis*, the blog of
IgnatianSpirituality.com

The Presence of God

Dear Lord, as I come to you today, fill my heart, my whole being, with the wonder of your presence. Help me remain receptive to you as I put aside the cares of this world. Fill my mind with your peace.

Freedom

Lord, grant me the grace to be free from the excesses of this life. Let me not get caught up with the desire for wealth. Keep my heart and mind free to love and serve you.

Consciousness

I exist in a web of relationships: links to nature, people, God.
I trace out these links, giving thanks for the life that flows through them.
Some links are twisted or broken; I may feel regret, anger, disappointment.
I pray for the gift of acceptance and forgiveness.

The Word

God speaks to each of us individually. I listen attentively to hear what he is saying to me. Read the text a few times; then listen. (Please turn to the Scripture on the following pages. Inspiration points are there, should you need them. When you are ready, return here to continue.)

Conversation

Jesus, you speak to me through the words of the Gospels. May I respond to your call today. Teach me to recognize your hand at work in my daily living.

Conclusion

I thank God for these moments we have spent together and for any insights I have been given concerning the text.

Sunday 21st April
Easter Sunday of the Resurrection of the Lord

John 20:1–9

Early on the first day of the week, while it was still dark, Mary Magdalene came to the tomb and saw that the stone had been removed from the tomb. So she ran and went to Simon Peter and the other disciple, the one whom Jesus loved, and said to them, "They have taken the Lord out of the tomb, and we do not know where they have laid him." Then Peter and the other disciple set out and went toward the tomb. The two were running together, but the other disciple outran Peter and reached the tomb first. He bent down to look in and saw the linen wrappings lying there, but he did not go in. Then Simon Peter came, following him, and went into the tomb. He saw the linen wrappings lying there, and the cloth that had been on Jesus' head, not lying with the linen wrappings but rolled up in a place by itself. Then the other disciple, who reached the tomb first, also went in, and he saw and believed; for as yet they did not understand the scripture, that he must rise from the dead.

- Mary went to do her best, to tend to Jesus' mortal remains. She accepted the reality as she saw it but was determined to do what she could to bring dignity and honor to her loved one and her teacher. Help me, O God, to do what I can as I remain alert, noticing the movement of your Spirit. May I receive life as you offer it, even if in unexpected ways.

- As described by Benedict XVI in his Easter Vigil homily, April 15, 2006, "The Resurrection was like an explosion of light," a "cosmic event" linking heaven and earth. But above all, it was "an explosion of love." "It ushered in a new dimension of being . . . through which a new world emerges." It is a "leap in the history of 'evolution' and of life in general towards a new future life, a new world which, starting from Christ, already continuously permeates this world of ours, transforms it, and draws it to itself." The Resurrection unites us with God and others. "If we live in this way, we transform the world." I sit with this paragraph and allow it to become my prayer.

Suscipe

Take, Lord, and receive all my liberty,
my memory, my understanding,
and my entire will,

all I have and call my own.
You have given all to me.

To you, Lord, I return it.
Everything is yours; do with it what you will.
Give me only your love and your grace;
that is enough for me.

—St. Ignatius of Loyola

Prayer to Know God's Will

May it please the supreme and divine Goodness
To give us all abundant grace
Ever to know his most holy will
And perfectly to fulfill it.

—St. Ignatius of Loyola